INTRODUCTION

Your toddler is growing out of the regular baby meals and you are worried about the next step? First, congratulations, you both are doing well. Second, you don't have to worry. This book in your hands provides the answers. I know because I have used the tricks in this book as a guide for feeding my daughter, Flo. Let me tell you a little story.

When it comes to feeding, my two children were raised in different ways. With my first, Brian, I did not go the extra mile to ensure that he was getting different varieties of food early on. He would not take anything else that I didn't wean him with, so I was always feeding him. Even at four, he still asks: "Mummy can you feed me?" However, with Flo, we started weaning her as soon as she was six months old, with baby-led weaning. Today, she knows the types of food she likes, she eats by herself and we don't have to feed her. In *What Flo Eats I,* I wrote about this experience with Flo. However, in *What Flo Eats II* which is in your hands, I write specifically about easy-to-prepare recipes.

Earlier in 2020, I organised weaning workshops for mothers, sharing practical steps on how to easily wean their babies. During the workshop, it was clear that many mothers were quite busy, making it difficult to invest the time meal planning and actual cooking demands. I understand that cooking homemade meals—morning, afternoon and evening, every day, seven days a week—can be hectic even for the finest parents. You know you should cook fresh meals for your little one but where is the time? In this book, I share with you Flo's favourite meals over the years, meal plans and snack ideas.

The book is broken into breakfast, lunch and dinner so it not only makes it easy for you to plan your cooking but also your food shopping in a way that you use fresh ingredients and nothing goes to waste. For breakfast, your little one can have grilled sandwich and fruits; for lunch, you can cook pasta in lentil sauce, mackerel and kiwi; while dinner can be chilli con carne, mash and broccoli. This book will save you time as you are not spending hours thinking of what to eat even before cooking. It will also save you money: time is money. Eating healthy meals keeps you child healthy and away from the hospital.

With a baby like Flo, I had to be creative, always thinking up the next creative food idea. I have written this book to save you the hassle of racking your head. Each recipe has been carefully crafted from personal experience as well as trial and error. However, you should also feel free to switch things up according to your baby's tastes. By offering a diverse menu of healthy meals, you can rest assured that your little one will benefit from a varied, tried and tested diet. What more? The meals are balanced, easy-to-cook and packed with nutrients. Your child loves veggies? Your child loves finger foods? In need of kid-friendly yet nutritious snack ideas? What Flo Eats II has you covered.

Each page of this book has a colourful picture of each meal that may entice your child to eat the book literally. Don't let them! What Flo Eats is filled with colourful yet nourishing meals, tasty yet healthy snacks that will appeal to your little one's senses and enhance physical development. So, the book contains options that appeal to young child's varying tastes. What Flo Eats II, your ultimate baby food guide includes:

- 75 FOOD RECIPES
- 25 SNACK IDEAS
- 4-WEEK MEAL PLAN
- OVER 10 VEGETARIAN MEALS

Your journey to a healthier food plan for your baby has just started but it does not end here. Want to learn more about Flo's latest food discoveries? Want to buy a "Growing with Flo" plate or bib? In search of a community to share your cooking experiences with? Then, join Flo here:

Instagram:
https://www.instagram.com/growingwithflo_/

Website:
https://www.growingwithflo.co.uk/

Email:
hello@growingwithflo.co.uk

BREAKFAST

1. English Breakfast Eggs and Beans

Serves 2

Ingredients
- 2 eggs
- ¼ medium onion, chopped
- 1 medium can baked beans (250g)
- 3 tablespoons olive oil
- Salt to taste

To serve
- 2 tomatoes, sliced
- 1 kiwi
- 1 toast (optional)

Method
- Heat up a saucepan, add oil and chopped onions, fry on medium heat for 3 minutes. Beat eggs and add a pinch of salt. Add beaten eggs, mix gently, then add in baked beans. Allow to cook and serve with tomatoes and kiwi.

2. Veggie Egg Frittata Served with Bread and Tomatoes (V)

Serves 2

Ingredients
- 3 eggs

- 150g green beans, chopped
- 2 green onions, chopped
- Salt
- Black pepper
- 2 tablespoons butter
- 1 seasoning cube
- Tomatoes, to serve
- 1 bagel, to serve

Method
- In a saucepan, add butter, green onions, green beans, seasoning cube and fry for 5 minutes. Meanwhile, break eggs in a bowl and whisk.
- Add salt and pepper to the veggies and mix well. Pour whisked eggs over the veggies and cover with a lid. Reduce heat and allow to cook. Once the eggs are cooked, cut into strips and serve with half a bagel and tomatoes.

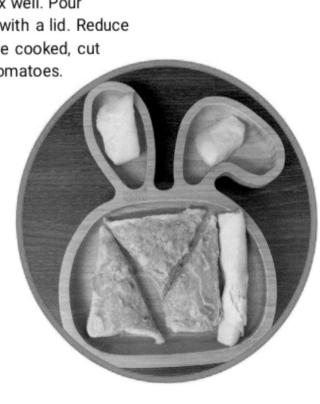

3. Avocado Toast with Chicken and Melon

Serves 2

Ingredients
- 2 slices of bread
- 1 avocado, mashed
- Sandwich chicken, 1 slice
- Melon, to serve

Method

- Toast bread and spread the mashed avocado on it. Serve with chicken and fruits.

4. Banana Pancake with Yoghurt and Kiwi

Serves 2

Ingredients

- 1 banana, mashed
- 1 egg
- ½ cup of flour
- 1 teaspoon vanilla extract
- 1 cup of milk
- 2 tablespoons of cooking oil

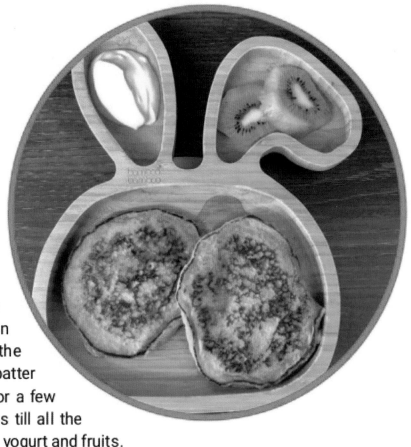

Method

- Add all ingredients together in a bowl and whisk to make a batter. Coat pan with 1 teaspoon of oil and scoop in some of the pancake batter. Once the batter starts to bubble, flip and fry for a few minutes. Continue this process till all the batter is fried. Serve with syrup, yogurt and fruits.

5. Breakfast Banana Muffin

Serves 6

Ingredients
- 1 cup oat bran
- 2 tablespoons cinnamon
- 3/4 cup skimmed milk
- 2 medium ripe bananas
- 2/3 cup brown/coconut sugar
- 4 tablespoons of coconut oil
- 2 teaspoons vanilla extract
- 2 eggs
- 2 cups flour
- 1 tablespoon baking powder
- 1 teaspoon baking soda

Method
- Preheat the oven to 350 and line muffin pan with paper muffin cups.
- Mash bananas in a bowl, add brown sugar, coconut oil, vanilla extract, eggs, and beat well together.
- In another bowl, mix 2 teaspoons of oat bran, 1 teaspoon of cinnamon, and set aside for the topping. Place the remaining oat bran in a bowl with the milk and leave to soak for 5 minutes. Sieve flour, baking powder, baking soda, and remaining cinnamon into a large bowl. In the flour mixture, stir in the soaked oat bran and the banana mixture. Mix lightly but thoroughly, just until smooth.
- Spoon the mixture into the paper cups and bake for 25-30 minutes or until well risen and golden brown. Lift the muffins out onto a wire rack to cool a little. Enjoy!

6. Chocolate Muffins

Serves 6

Ingredients

- 2 cups whole wheat flour
- 1/2 cup cocoa powder
- 1 tablespoon baking powder
- 1/2 tablespoon baking soda
- Pinch of salt
- 2 ripe bananas
- 2 eggs
- 30g coconut oil/butter
- 113g maple syrup
- 1 cup of full cream milk

Method

- Preheat oven at 200 degrees. Mix the dry ingredients together in a bowl and set aside. Mash the bananas in another bowl, break the eggs into the bowl and mix both together. Add milk, maple and coconut oil, then stir. Then add in dry ingredients, stir and place in your muffin cups/ liners. Top with chocolate buttons and bake for 30 minutes or more if required.
- Let it cool down before serving. Serve alone or with Greek yogurt.

7. Cheesy Egg-roll and Croissant with Fruits

Serves 2

Ingredients
- 2 eggs, whisked
- 2 tablespoons grated cheese
- Salt
- ¼ cup peas
- Pepper
- 1 tablespoon butter
- Croissant, to serve
- Strawberries, to serve

Method
- Heat a non-stick pan, add butter and allow to melt. Swirl round to ensure the butter covers the pan. Add salt and pepper to whisked eggs.
- Pour whisked eggs in the buttered pan, add peas and allow to cook on low heat for 3 minutes. Sprinkle cheese on the egg and gently roll up the eggs. Reduce heat, cover the pan and leave to simmer for a few minutes.
- Serve eggs with croissant and strawberries.

8. Raspberry and Oats Smoothie

Serves 2

Ingredients
- ¼ cup oats

- ½ cup raspberries
- 1 cup milk
- ½ banana
- 1 teaspoon chia seeds

Method
Blend all ingredients together and serve.

9. French Toast with Berries

Serves 2

Ingredients
- 2 slices of bread
- 1 teaspoon cinnamon
- 1 egg
- Pinch of salt
- Pinch of black pepper
- ¼ cup whole milk
- 1 tablespoon butter
- 1 tablespoon maple syrup or honey
- Berries, to serve

Method
- Break egg in a bowl, add cinnamon, salt, pepper, milk, and whisk till combined. Heat up butter in a pan, dip bread in egg mixture till evenly coated. Fry bread in buttered pan for about 5 minutes till bread is brown. Flip halfway to cook

both sides. Serve with a drizzle of maple syrup or honey with berries.

10. Veggie Fish Cake

Serves 5

Ingredients

- 350g cooked mackerel or salmon, flaked
- 1 tablespoon flour
- ½ cup peas
- ½ cup broccoli, chopped
- 1 cup cooked potatoes
- 1 egg
- Salt
- 3 tablespoons of olive oil
- Pinch of black pepper

Method

- Mash cooked potatoes roughly, combine all other ingredients except oil with the mashed potatoes. Divide batter into 5 and shape into patties. Fry in oil for 5 minutes on each side. Serve with fruits.

11. Pancakes, Eggs and Fruits

Serves 2

Ingredients

- 3 eggs

- ½ cup self-raising flour
- 1 teaspoon vanilla extract
- 1 cup of milk
- 1 tablespoon sugar
- 2 tablespoons oil
- 1 tablespoon butter
- Salt
- Pepper

Method

- In a bowl, combine flour, 1 egg, sugar, and milk. Whisk till smooth. Oil pan lightly and fry batter by scooping the batter using a small cup or scoop. Flip after a few minutes and repeat the process till the batter is used up.
- In the same pan, add butter. Whisk the remaining eggs, add salt and pepper and a splash milk. Fry in butter and scramble till cooked.
- Serve pancakes with scrambled eggs and fruits of choice.

12. Berry Milkshake (V)

Serves 2

Ingredients
- ½ cup of oats
- 1 handful berries
- 1 tablespoon peanut butter or flax seed

- 1 cup almond milk

Method
Blend all ingredients together and enjoy.

13. Creamy Banana Oats with Berries

Serves 2

Ingredients
- 1/2 cup oats
- 1/2 cup water
- 1/2 cup milk
- 1 medium banana, mashed
- A handful raspberries

Method
- There are two ways of preparing oats: On the stovetop or in the microwave. I usually cook mine in the microwave to save time. Combine oats, and your liquid in a bowl, and microwave it for about 2 minutes, or according to package directions. If your oats is too thick, stir in a little bit more milk or water. Add mashed banana and stir. Top with berries. Enjoy!

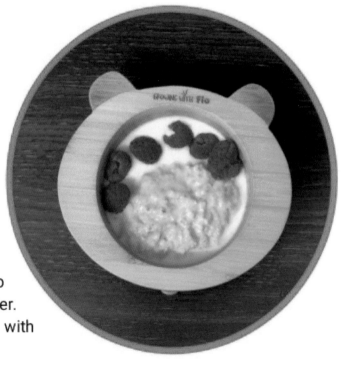

14. Protein Porridge Breakfast

Serves 2

Ingredients
- 1/2 cup oats
- 1/2 cup water
- 1/2 cup milk
- 1 tablespoon peanut butter or 1 teaspoon chia seeds
- 1 tablespoon honey
- 1 boiled egg

Method
- There are two ways of preparing oats: On the stovetop or in the microwave. I usually cook mine in the microwave to save time. Combine oats, milk, water, peanut butter/ chia seeds in a bowl, and microwave it for 2 minutes, or according to package directions. If your oat is too thick, stir in a little bit more milk or water. Top with boiled eggs. Enjoy!

15. Grilled Sandwich

Serves 2

Ingredients

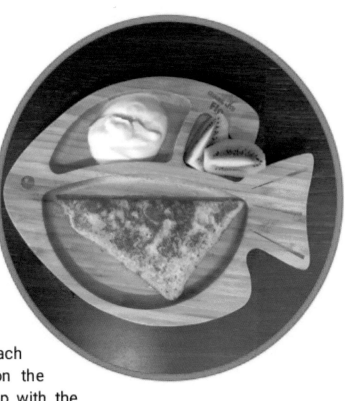

- 2 slices of bread
- 2 tablespoons peanut butter
- 1 medium banana, sliced
- 1 teaspoon butter
- 1/3 cup yogurt
- 1 kiwi

Method

- Heat a pan or skillet over medium heat, add butter.
- Spread peanut butter on one side of each sliced bread. Place banana slices on the peanut buttered side of one slice, top with the other slice and press together firmly. Pan-fry the sandwich until golden brown on each side, about 2 minutes per side. Serve with kiwi and yoghurt.

16. Chocolate Muffin

Serves 6

Ingredients

- 2 cups whole wheat flour
- 1/2 cup cocoa powder
- 1 tablespoon baking powder
- 1/2 tablespoon baking soda
- Pinch of salt
- 2 ripe bananas
- 2 eggs
- 30g coconut oil/butter
- 113g maple syrup
- 1 cup of full milk

Method

- Preheat oven at 200 degrees. Mix the dry ingredients together in a bowl and set aside. Mash the bananas in another bowl, break the eggs into the bowl and mix both together. Add milk, maple and coconut oil, then stir. Then add in dry ingredients, stir and place in your muffin cups/ liners. Top with chocolate buttons and bake for 30 minutes or more if required.
- Serve alone or with Greek yogurt.
- Let it cool down before serving.

17. Banana Bread

Serves 10

Ingredients
- 3 medium ripe bananas
- 2 eggs
- ½ cup plain Greek yogurt/whole milk
- 1/3 cup honey/maple syrup
- 1 teaspoon vanilla extract
- 1 teaspoon baking soda
- 2 cups wheat flour

Method
- Preheat the oven to 350.
- In a bowl, mash bananas. In another bowl, mix eggs, milk, honey, vanilla extract, and baking soda. Add the wheat flour and mix. Pour the mix into a greased 9x5-inch bread pan. Bake for about 50-60 minutes, or until a toothpick comes out clean from the middle of the bread. Keep an eye on the bread so it doesn't burn. Serve with smoothie of choice.

18. Avocado Smoothie

Serves 1

Ingredients
- 1/4 avocado
- 1/4 cup plain Greek yoghurt
- 1 apple
- Thumb sized ginger
- 1 banana
- 1 teaspoon honey
- Pinch of cinnamon

Method
- Blend all ingredients together with 1 cup of water and serve.

19. Egg and Avocado Wrap

Serves 2

Ingredients
- 2 eggs
- 1 medium avocado, sliced
- 1 teaspoon oil
- 1 tomato, chopped
- 1 teaspoon ground pepper or black pepper
- 1 teaspoon lemon juice
- 1 tortilla wrap
- Salt to taste

Method

- In a bowl, break eggs and whisk, add salt and pepper to taste. Heat up oil in a pan, add whisked eggs, and tomatoes. Cook for 5 minutes. Season with more salt and pepper if required.
- Add lemon juice to avocado and set aside.
- Spread egg and tomato mixture on tortilla wrap, add avocado and roll up the wrap very tightly. Wrap in a cling film or foil paper and serve warm.

20. Chocolate Smoothie

Serves 2

Ingredients
- 1/4 cup of peanuts / 2 tablespoons peanut butter
- 1 tablespoon cocoa powder
- 1/3 Greek yoghurt/whole milk
- 1 banana
- 1 teaspoon honey

Method
- Blend all together with 1 cup of water

and enjoy!

21. Blueberry Smoothie

Serves 2

Ingredients
- 1 handful blueberries
- ½ cup mango
- 1 apple
- 1 tablespoon ginger
- 1 cup water

Method
- Wash, chop and blend all ingredients together with some ice and enjoy.

22. Mangonana

Serves 2

Ingredients
- 1 mango
- 2 bananas
- 1 peach
- 4 tablespoons natural yoghurt

Method

- Wash and chop fruits. Blend till smooth and enjoy

23. Oatmeal Pancakes with Yoghurt

Serves 2

Ingredients
- ½ cup yogurt
- 1/4 cup oat flour
- 1/2 cup wheat flour
- 1 teaspoon sugar
- 1 teaspoon baking powder
- 1 teaspoon ground cinnamon
- 1 egg
- 1 tablespoon coconut oil
- 1 handful blueberries

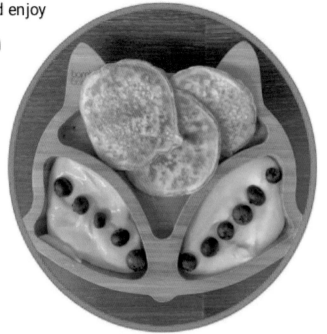

Method
- Mix blended oats, brown sugar, baking powder, salt, and cinnamon together in a bowl.
- Whisk eggs, coconut oil, and yogurt together in a separate bowl. Mix oat mixture and egg mixture with the flour, stir to combine. Spray oil on a griddle or skillet over medium heat; pour about 1/4 cup batter into the hot skillet.
- Cook pancakes for a few minutes, until bubbles appear on top layer. Flip and cook the other side until evenly browned, about a few more minutes. Serve with fruit and

yoghurt.

24. Egg and Potato Medley with Strawberries

Serves 4

Ingredients
- 4 eggs
- 2 green and red bell peppers, diced
- 2 tomatoes, chopped
- 3 medium potatoes, cubed
- 3 tablespoons cooking oil
- 1 onion, chopped
- 1 seasoning cube
- 1 teaspoon chilli pepper (optional)
- Salt
- Strawberries

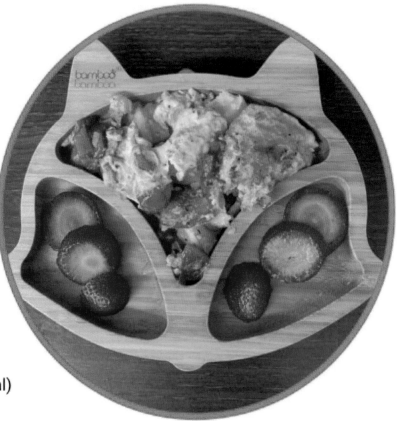

Method
- In a pot, add potatoes, salt and 2 cups of water. Cook for 10 minutes, drain in a colander, and set aside.
- Heat a pan on medium heat, add oil and onions with a pinch of salt. Allow to cook for a few minutes. Add chopped tomatoes and peppers, stir frequently for 4 minutes. Add cooked potatoes, chilli, seasoning cube and stir. In a bowl, break eggs and whisk. Add to the sauce and stir, reduce heat, and cover pan with a lid. Cook for 5 to 7 minutes or till egg mixture is cooked.
- Serve with strawberries.

25. Greenhouse Smoothie

Serves 2

Ingredients

- 1 cup pinepple
- Handfull spinach
- 1 banana
- 1 cup wholemilk

Method

Blend all ingredients together and serve.

LUNCH

1. Beans Pottage with Plantain

Serves 5 to 7

Ingredients

- 2.5 cups honey beans
- ¼ cups palm oil
- 2 red bell peppers
- 1 scotch bonnet (optional)
- 1 onion
- ¼ cup ground crayfish
- 2 medium plantain
- ½ cup cooking oil (to fry plantain)
- Salt to taste

Method

- Boil beans by adding water double the size of the beans. Cook for 30 minutes, or till soft. Blend bell peppers, scotch bonnet and onion together.
- Once the beans is almost cooked, add blended pepper mix, crayfish and salt. Add water if required and cook on medium heat. Cook for another 15 to 20 minutes or till very soft.
- Meanwhile, in a frying pan, heat up oil. Peel the skin off the plantain and cut into cubes. Once the oil is hot, add plantain. While frying, turn plantain at intervals until golden, for about 8 minutes. Serve beans with plantain.

2. Moimoi with Steamed Veggies

Serves 7

Ingredients

- 2.5 cups beans (brown or white)
- 1 chopped onion
- 2 large red bell peppers
- 1 small pointed pepper
- 2 scotch bonnet peppers
- 4 eggs (3 boiled, 1 fresh)
- ¼ cup coconut oil
- 200g cooked mackerel, flaked
- 1 seasoning cube
- 2 teaspoons salt

Method

- Soak beans in hot water for easy peeling.
- Add all peppers, onion with 500ml water (or stock) in a blender and blend till batter is very smooth.
- Pour the batter into a large bowl, break in 1 fresh egg, add the coconut oil, seasoning cube, salt and mix batter well.
- In a baking dish or ramekins, add a teaspoon of oil to coat it evenly. Fill the ramekins or baking dish with up to ¾ of the batter, and top with the mackerel.
- Preheat oven to 200 degrees. Bake for 45 minutes and enjoy! Serve with boiled eggs and steamed veggies.

Steam option

- Boil some water in a deep pot.

- Fill the ramekin with the batter, cover and set into the pot. Steam for 45 minutes and serve with boiled eggs and steamed veggies.

3. Pasta in Lentil Sauce Served with Mackerel and Kiwi

Serves 6

Ingredients
- 100g red split lentil
- 300g pasta
- 2 bell peppers
- 1 scotch bonnet (optional)
- 3 medium tomatoes
- 1 onion, chopped
- ¼ cup olive oil
- 2 cups stock (chicken or vegetable)
- 1 clove garlic, minced
- 1 tablespoon ginger, minced
- 1 teaspoon salt
- 300g cooked mackerel, to serve
- Kiwi, to serve

Method
- Blend tomatoes, bell peppers and scotch bonnet and set aside.
- Heat up oil and add chopped onion, garlic and ginger. Fry on medium heat for 2 minutes. Add blended pepper mix and cook for 5 to 7 minutes, stirring occasionally.
- Add stock and bring to a boil, then add washed lentil and salt. Cover

and cook for 10 minutes or till lentil is soft. Add in the pasta and top with water enough to cover the pasta.

- Leave to cook for 10 to 12 minutes or till the pasta is soft and serve with kiwi and mackerel.

4. Macaroni and Chickpea Casserole Served with Yoghurt and Steamed Carrots (V)

Serves 6 to 7

Ingredients

- 1 can cooked chickpea (350g)
- 300g macaroni
- 2 bell peppers
- 1 scotch bonnet (optional)
- 3 medium tomatoes
- 1 onion, chopped
- ¼ cup olive oil
- 1 cup stock (chicken or vegetable)
- 1 teaspoon smoked paprika
- 1 tablespoon tomato puree
- 1 teaspoon oregano
- 1 teaspoon salt
- Greek yogurt, to serve
- Steamed carrot, to serve

Method

- Cook pasta in salted water for 12 minutes or till cooked. Blend

tomatoes, bell pepper and scotch bonnet.
- Heat up oil and add chopped onion, oregano and smoked paprika. Fry on medium heat for 1 minute and add tomato puree. Mix till well combined and add blended pepper mix. Cook for 5 to 7 minutes, stirring occasionally. Add chickpea and stock. Bring to a boil, then add drained macaroni. Cover and cook for 5 minutes.
- Serve with steamed carrot and yoghurt.

5. Veggie Coconut Rice and Egg (V)

Serves 5 to 6

Ingredients
- 300g rice
- 1 tablespoon curry powder
- 1 teaspoon thyme
- 1 onion chopped
- 2 cups mixed vegetables
- 1 scotch bonnet
- 1 tablespoon ginger, minced
- 1 can coconut milk (400g)
- 3 tablespoons coconut oil
- 1 teaspoon white pepper
- 1 teaspoon black pepper
- 2 cups stock
- 1 seasoning cube

Method
- Heat up oil in a pan, add chopped onion, thyme, white pepper, black pepper and fry for 3 to 5 minutes. Add coconut milk, stock and seasoning cube. Bring to a boil. Wash rice, then add to the pot. Cover and cook for 25 minutes, or till rice is cooked. Add veggies and mix with the rice, then cover it. Serve with boiled eggs and cucumber.

6. Rice and Chickpea Sauce (V)

Serves 6

Ingredients

- 350g rice
- 1 can coconut milk
- 1 can chickpea
- 3 medium-sized potatoes, peeled and diced
- 1 tablespoon curry powder
- 1 clove of garlic, minced
- 1 tablespoon ginger, minced
- 1 cup stock
- 1 bell pepper, chopped
- 1 onion, diced
- ¼ cup coconut oil
- 1 teaspoon paprika
- Salt

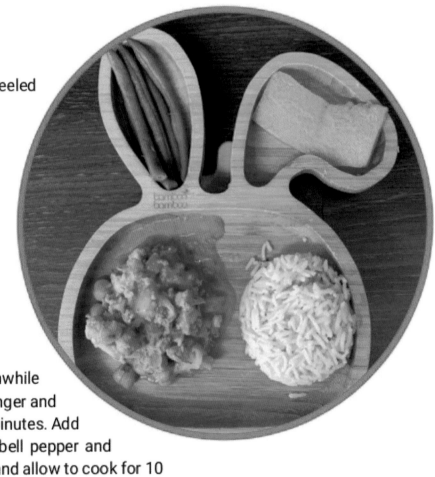

Method

- Cook rice and set aside. Meanwhile heat oil in a pan, add onion, ginger and fry on medium heat for a few minutes. Add garlic, paprika, curry powder, bell pepper and potatoes. Add a cup of stock and allow to cook for 10 minutes. Add chickpea and coconut milk, allow to simmer for 10 minutes. Serve with rice and steamed veggies

7. Creamy Mushroom Pasta with Meat balls and Mango

Serves 6

Ingredients

- 300g pasta
- 1 cup mushroom, diced
- 250g cream (single or double)
- 1 clove garlic
- 1 bell pepper, diced
- 1 onion, diced
- 1 seasoning cube
- 3 tablespoons olive oil
- Salt and pepper to taste
- Cooked meat ball, to serve
- Serve with sliced mango

Method

- Cook pasta in a pot of salted water for 12 minutes or according to the instruction on the packet. Drain and set aside.
- In a pan, heat up oil, add onion and garlic.
- Fry on medium heat for 30 seconds, then add the pepper and mushroom, stir fry for 5 minutes then add seasoning cube, salt and pepper. Cook for a few minutes and add the cream. Followed by the pasta. If the pasta is still hard, add some of the pasta water to loosen up cream. Once you are happy with the consistency, take off heat and serve with meat ball and mango.

8. Eba and Egusi Soup

Serves 7

Ingredients

- 2.5 cups egusi, dry milled
- 1/3 cup palm oil
- 700g fish
- ¼ cup crayfish
- 1 tablespoon locust beans (optional)
- 3 bell peppers
- 700g green leafy vegetables of choice, chopped
- 1 scotch bonnet pepper
- 1 seasoning cube
- Salt to taste

Method

- Blend bell pepper, scotch bonnet and onion together. Heat up palm oil; add in boiled pepper mix. Cook for 10 minutes or till pepper mix is cooked. Add seasoning cube, locust beans and salt to taste. Add fish and allow to cook for 10 minutes. Add half cup of water to the blended egusi to dissolve it. Add it to the pepper mix and some water or stock. Cover and cook on low heat for another 10 minutes. Be careful while stirring so as not to break the fish.
- The soup might be too thick, add water to it according to your preference. Once the egusi is cooked, add chopped vegetables, and allow to simmer.
- Serve with eba (garri cooked in boiling water).

9. Giant Couscous and Veggie Medley

Serves 6

Ingredients
- 2.5 cups giant couscous
- 3.5 cups tomato stew
- 3 .5 cups of stock
- 1 scotch bonnet pepper, diced
- 2 cloves of garlic, minced
- 1 tablespoon ginger, minced.
- 1 medium onion, chopped
- 1 seasoning cube
- 1 teaspoon thyme
- 150g green beans
- 2 teaspoons curry powder
- 2 bay leaves
- Salt to taste

Method
- Add stock, tomato stew and boil in a large saucepan. Add couscous, curry powder, thyme, bay leaves, garlic, ginger, onion, pepper, and salt to taste.
- Cover the pot and leave to cook on low to medium heat so couscous does not burn. Cook for 20 minutes or till couscous is tender. Add green beans 5 minutes before taking the couscous off heat.

10. Mexican Pasta Mix with Fruits and Egg

Serves 3

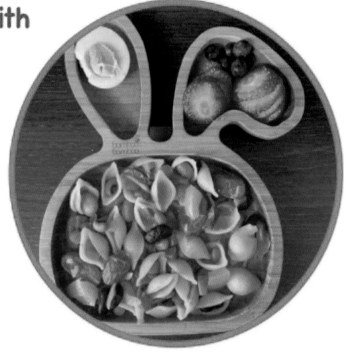

Ingredients

- 300g cooked pasta
- 1 can mixed beans
- 1 bell pepper, chopped
- 1 teaspoon Mexican spice
- 2 tomatoes, chopped
- 1 onion, chopped
- 3 tablespoons olive oil

Method

- Heat oil in a pan, add onion and fry for a few minutes. Add chopped tomatoes, beans and bell pepper. Add salt and mix till combined. Add the cooked pasta.
- Serve with boiled eggs and strawberries.

11. Quick Pepperoni Pizza with Steamed Broccoli and Yoghurt

Serves 4

Ingredients

- 1 ready to roll pizza dough or 2 flatbreads
- 4 tablespoons tomato sauce
- 10 slices pepperoni
- ¼ cup grated cheese
- 1 floret steamed broccoli, to serve
- Yoghurt, to serve

Method

- Preheat oven at 200 degrees. Roll pizza dough, if using. Spread tomato sauce on the rolled pizza dough or flat bread. Top with cheese and pepperoni.
- Bake in the oven. If using pizza dough, bake for 20 to 25 minutes. If using flatbread, bake for 10 minutes. Served with steamed broccoli and yoghurt

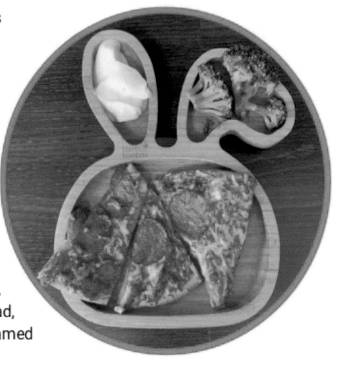

12. Jollof Rice, Chicken and Avocado

Serves 5 to 6

Ingredients

- 2.5 cups long grain rice
- 3.5 cups tomato stew
- 3 .5 cups of stock
- 1 scotch bonnet pepper
- 2 garlic cloves, minced
- 1 tablespoon ginger, minced.
- 1 medium onion, chopped
- 1 seasoning cube1 teaspoon thyme
- 150g green beans
- 2 teaspoons curry powder
- 2 bay leaves
- Salt to taste
- Avocado, to serve
- Chicken wings, to serve

Method

- Parboil the rice, drain in a sieve and set aside. Add stock, tomato stew and boil in a large saucepan. Add parboiled rice, curry powder, thyme, bay leaves, garlic, ginger, onion, pepper, and salt to taste.
- Cover the pot and leave to cook on low to medium heat, so rice does not burn. Cook for 20 minutes, or till rice is tender. Serve with chicken wings and avocado.

13. Grilled Chicken Wings, Plantain, and Grapes

Serves 7

Ingredients

- 1kg fresh chicken/turkey
- 3 garlic cloves, minced
- 1 tablespoon crushed ginger
- 1 tablespoon curry
- 1 tablespoon thyme
- 1 tablespoon rosemary
- 1 tablespoon salt
- 1 seasoning cube
- 1 large onion, chopped
- 1 tablespoon ground pepper
- 700g plantain.

Method

- Wash chicken wings and pat dry with kitchen paper towels and set aside. In a big bowl, add salt, thyme, curry, rosemary, seasoning cube, garlic, onions, and black pepper. Add chicken, cover, and leave in the fridge overnight.
- If you're in a hurry, let it marinate for 2-3 hours. Pre-heat oven for 10 minutes and grill chicken for 40 minutes, turning halfway through. Serve with fried plantain and grapes

14. Grilled Avocado Tortilla Wrap with Cucumber and Orange

Serves 2

Ingredients

- 1 tortilla wrap
- 1 tomato, chopped
- 100g cooked chicken
- ½ avocado, mashed
- Sliced cucumbers, to serve
- 1 orange, to serve

Method

- Layer the tomatoes, avocado and chicken on the wrap. Fold the wrap into a pocket and grill for 6 to 8 minutes or you can use a frying pan by frying both sides till crispy in a non-stick pot with a teaspoon oil. Serve with cucumbers and orange

15. Broccoli and Prawn Rice

Serves 5 to 6

Ingredients

- 350g prawn
- 2 cups broccoli floret
- 1 cup baby carrots
- 300g short grain/ easy cook rice
- 1 onion, chopped
- 2 tablespoons coconut oil
- 1 teaspoon ginger, minced
- 1 garlic clove, minced
- 1 teaspoon black pepper
- 1 seasoning cube
- 1 teaspoon thyme
- 1 bell pepper, diced
- 3 cups chicken stock

Method

- Heat a non stick pan over medium heat, add a tablespoon of oil. Sprinkle salt and pepper on prawns. Fry for 5 minutes and set aside (skip this if using cooked prawns).
- Add remaining oil to the pan, add onion, garlic, ginger, pepper black pepper, thyme, and fry for a few minutes. Add carrots, broccoli, seasoning cube and stock. Bring to boil, then easy cook rice.
- Cook for 20 minutes till soft, stir in cooked prawns and serve.

16. Rice and Beans with Fish Stew

Serves 6

Ingredients
- 2 cups honey beans
- 1.5 cups rice
- ¼ cup cooking oil
- 2 large onions
- 4 tomatoes
- 1 scotch bonnet pepper
- 1 cup stock
- Salt
- 3 bell peppers
- 1 seasoning cube
- 300g fish

Method
- Boil 3 cups of water in a pot; add rinsed beans and cook for 15 minutes. Meanwhile rinse rice till water runs clear, add to the beans and top up with water if required, add salt and cook further for 20 to 25 minutes or till rice and beans is soft. Set aside.
- Meanwhile, blend tomatoes, onion, peppers together and boil for 15 minutes. In a separate pot, add cooking oil. Once oil is hot, add boiled pepper mix, salt, seasoning cube, stock and fish. Cook for 25 to 30 minutes and serve with rice and beans and a side dish of vegetables.

17. Chickpea Curry with Rice (V)

Serves 6

Ingredients

- 500g chickpea
- 1 can coconut milk
- 1 glove garlic, minced
- 1 teaspoon ginger paste
- ½ teaspoon ground turmeric
- 2 bell peppers, diced
- 1 onion, diced
- 1 teaspoon garam masala
- 1 tablespoon curry powder
- 1.5 cup vegetable stock
- Salt
- 1 tablespoon coconut oil
- 1 cup diced tomatoes
- Black pepper

Method

- Blend bell pepper and tomatoes and set aside. In a pan, heat coconut oil, add diced onion and cook till onion is softened, stir frequently. Add garlic, ginger, garam masala and curry powder. Cook on low heat for 30 seconds before adding pepper blend. Add salt, black pepper and allow to cook for 7 minutes, stirring frequently.
- Add drained chickpea, stock and leave to simmer for 5 to 7 minutes. Stir in coconut milk. Reduce heat and simmer for further 10 minutes, or till sauce thickens and reduce reduced. Serve with rice and a side of vegetables and lemon wedge (optional).

18. Giant Couscous Stir-fry

Serves 5 to 6

Ingredients

- 350g giant couscous
- 1 tablespoon curry powder
- 1 teaspoon thyme
- 1 onion chopped
- 2 cups mixed veg
- 3 tablespoons cooking oil
- 1 teaspoon white pepper
- 1 teaspoon black pepper
- 2 cups stock
- 1 seasoning cube
- Grilled chicken, to serve

Method

- Cook couscous in stock and one cup of water for 20 minutes, or till rice is cooked.
- Heat oil in a pan, add chopped onion, thyme, white pepper and black pepper, reduce heat to medium and fry for 3 minutes. Add mixed vegetables and seasoning cube. Fry for a few minutes.
- Add the cooked couscous to the veggie stir-fry, mix till combined. Add a splash of water, cover, and allow to simmer on low heat for 10 minutes. Serve with grilled chicken.

19. Sea Food Risotto with Meatballs and Fruits

Serves 5

Ingredients

- 500g seafood mix
- 1 onion, chopped
- 1 teaspoon white pepper
- 350g arborio rice (risotto)
- 2 cloves garlic, minced
- 1 cup peas
- 1 tablespoon olive oil
- 2 cups vegetable stock
- Meat balls
- Parsley to garnish

Method

- Heat oil in a pan, add onion and cook for 5 minutes. Add garlic and white pepper to the onion. Stir for a minute and add rice. Add a ladle of stock and mix the rice until bubbling, continue adding stock, one ladle at a time till the stock is exhausted.
- Continue stirring for 10 minutes. If the water dries up and the rice is quite hard, add in more water. Leave to cook for 10 minutes or till rice is soft. Add seafood and peas. Mix into the rice. Garnish with parsley, fruits, and meat balls.

20. Spaghetti Bolognese with Veggies

Serves 4

Ingredients

- 400g minced meat
- 2 cans chopped tomatoes (350g)
- 1 cup grated carrot
- 1 onion, chopped
- 2 tablespoons oil
- 1 teaspoon ginger, minced
- 1 teaspoon smoked paprika
- 1 seasoning cube
- 1 garlic clove, minced
- 1 teaspoon chilli flakes (optional)
- Salt to taste

Method

- Heat oil in a pot, add onion and ginger and allow to fry on medium heat for a few minutes.
- Add smoked paprika, garlic and cook for 30 seconds. Add minced meat. Cook till meat is browned and no longer red. Add grated carrots, chopped tomato, chilli flakes, seasoning cube, and half cup water.
- Cover the pot and leave simmer for 25 minutes or till sauce thickens. Serve with pasta, and a side of steamed veggies.

21. Jollof Bulgur, Peas and Wings

Serves 5

Ingredients

- 2.5 cups bulgur wheat
- 3.5 cups tomato stew
- 3 .5 cups of stock
- 1 scotch bonnet pepper
- 2 garlic cloves, minced
- 1 tablespoon minced ginger.
- 1 medium onion, chopped
- 1 seasoning cube1 teaspoon thyme
- 150g green beans
- 2 teaspoons curry powder
- 2 bay leaves
- Salt to taste
- Steamed peas, to serve
- Chicken wings, to serve
- Orange, to serve

Method

- Parboil the bulgur wheat, drain in a sieve, and set aside. Add stock, tomato stew and boil in a large saucepan. Add parboiled bulgur wheat, curry powder, thyme, bay leaves, garlic, ginger, onion, pepper, and salt to taste.
- Cover the pot and leave to cook on low to medium heat so bulgur wheat does not burn. Cook for 20 minutes or till bulgur wheat is tender. Serve with chicken wings, steamed peas and orange.

22. Cheesy Quesadilla

Serves 2

Ingredients
- 4 tablespoons bolognese sauce (see Lunch 20 for recipe)
- 2 tablespoons cheese
- 2 small tortilla wraps

Method
- Layer bolognese sauce on the tortilla wrap, covering half the wrap. Top with cheese and fold over the other half. Grill on each side for 5 minutes or till cheese is melted.
- You can also do this using a pan. Heat pan and add a teaspoon of oil; once hot, add the wrap to the pan using a spoon to hold down the wrap. Flip over once the cheese is melted and cook for 5 minutes on the other side. Serve with a side dish of fruits or veggies

23. Sweet Potato Pancakes (V)

Serves 2

Ingredients

- 1 cup baked/boiled sweet potatoes
- 1 cup all-purpose flour
- 180ml almond milk
- 1 tablespoon maple syrup
- 1 teaspoon coconut oil
- 1 teaspoon baking powder
- 1 teaspoon baking soda
- 1 teaspoon cinnamon

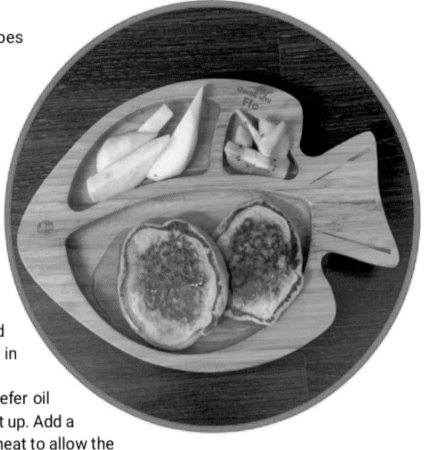

Method

- Mix flour, baking powder, baking soda, cinnamon in a bowl and set aside.
- Mash the sweet potatoes, add milk, maple, oil and mix. Fold in the flour and mix all together.
- Spray a frying pan with oil—I prefer oil sprays for pancakes—and heat it up. Add a little at a time and cook on low heat to allow the pancakes cook thoroughly. Let it cook until the middle becomes bubbly, then flip with a spatula till the other side is cooked. Serve with more maple syrup and enjoy!

24. Egg and Vegetable Cups Served with Fruits

Serves 6

Ingredients
- 6 eggs
- 1 red bell pepper
- 1 green bell pepper
- 1 onion
- 2 tomatoes
- 1 cup shredded cooked meat of choice (beef, chicken, bacon, etc.)
- 2 tablespoons cooking oil
- Salt and spices of choice to taste
- 1 cup cooked sweet potatoes, diced
- ¼ cup mozzarella cheese (optional)

Method
- Preheat oven at 200 °C. Chop all the vegetables.
- Add cooking oil to a non-stick frying pan. Once the oil is hot, add chopped onion and fry on low heat till soft (approximately 3 minutes). Add tomatoes and pepper.
- Fry the vegetable mix for 5 minutes while stirring frequently, add chilli and season with salt and pepper to taste.
- Add the potatoes and meat then mix all together. Once everything is well combined, take off the heat and set aside to cool.
- In a bowl, whisk the eggs and season to taste with salt and pepper.
- Pour the vegetable and meat mixture into whisked eggs and mix till well combined.
- Pour mixture into the baking cup tray (or cup cake tray) and top each cup with cheese

(optional).
- Bake in the oven for 15 mins. Serve with fruits of choice.

25. One-Pan Chicken Carrot Couscous

Serves 5

Ingredients
- 500g couscous
- 400g tomatoes, chopped
- 250g carrots, chopped
- 250g cooked chicken, chopped
- 2 tablespoons coconut oil
- 2 tablespoons tomato paste
- 2/12 cups of chicken stock
- 1 large bell pepper
- 1/2 chopped onion
- 2 crushed garlic cloves
- 1 tablespoon of fresh ginger
- Salt to taste

Method
- Heat the coconut oil in a large pan and cook the onion for about 2 minutes, or until softened. Add the carrots, bell peppers, chopped tomatoes and tomato paste. Cook for 2 minutes and add ginger, garlic, chicken and cook for 7-10 mins until the carrot is cooked.
- Add couscous, then pour the stock, salt and stir once. Cover with a lid or tightly cover the pan with foil and leave for about 10 minutes until the couscous has soaked up all the stock and is soft. Fluff up the couscous with a fork and serve.

DINNER

1. Chilli con Carne Served with Steamed Corn or Broccoli

Serves 6 to 8

Ingredients

- 400g minced meat
- 2 cans chopped tomatoes (350g)
- 1 cup kidney beans, cooked
- 2 cups mixed vegetables, fresh or frozen onion, chopped
- 2 tablespoons oil
- 1 teaspoon minced ginger
- 1 teaspoon smoked paprika
- 1 seasoning cube
- 1 teaspoon chilli flakes (optional)
- Salt to taste

Method

- Heat oil in a pot, add onion and ginger and allow to fry on medium heat for a few minutes.
- Add smoked paprika, then add minced meat. Cook till meat is browned and no longer red. Add chopped tomatoes, kidney beans, chilli flakes, seasoning cube, and half cup water.
- Cover the pot to simmer for 20 minutes. Add mixed vegetables and simmer for 10 minutes.

2. Creamy Mashed Potatoes

Serves 5

Ingredients

- 4 medium-sized potatoes, peeled and cubed
- ½ cup cream or full fat milk
- 2 tablespoons butter
- 1 teaspoon black pepper
- Salt to taste

Method

- Boil potato with salt. Drain water, add butter and black pepper.
- Mash with a potato masher then add cream or milk and mash till combined and smooth. Serve warm.

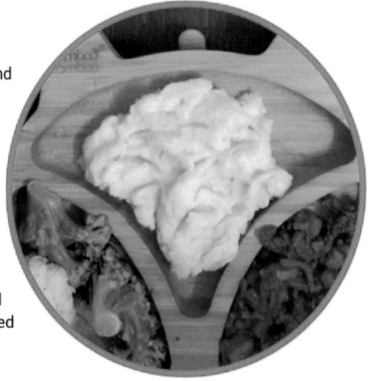

3. Pasta in Tomato Sauce and Boiled Egg

Serves 5 to 6

Ingredient

- 300g Pasta
- 1 can chopped tomatoes (400g)
- 1 onion, chopped
- 2 medium carrots, grated

- 1 medium-sized courgette, diced
- 1 teaspoon smoked paprika
- 1 teaspoon oregano
- 1 teaspoon black pepper
- ¼ cup olive oil
- 1 seasoning cube
- Salt to taste

Method

- Heat up oil, add chopped onion, oregano and paprika. Fry for a few minutes on medium heat and add chopped tomatoes, black pepper, and seasoning cube.
- Cook for 15 minutes and add grated carrots, courgette, and salt. Cook pasta in salted water till al-dente approximately 12 minutes, drain and set aside.
- Add pasta to the sauce and mix till combined, add some pasta water, if too dry. Serve with boiled egg.

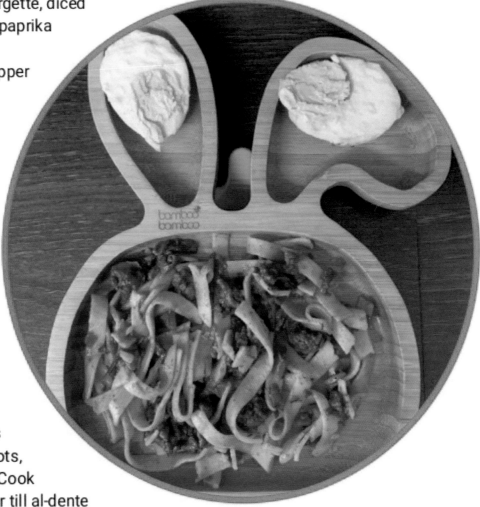

4. Grilled Platter: Sweet Potatoes, Mackerel and Veggies

Serves 5 to 6

Ingredients
- 4 medium-sized sweet potatoes
- 1 tablespoon black pepper
- 400g mackerel250g steamed carrots
- 1 avocado

Method
- Cut potatoes into wedges, rinse and pat dry. Season with salt, pepper and oil.
- Clean mackerel and season with salt and pepper. Grill mackerel and sweet potatoes in the oven for 25 to 30 minutes.
- Serve with steamed carrots and avocado.

5. Curried Bulgur Wheat Served with Chicken and Green Beans

Ingredients

- 500g boneless chicken, cut into strips
- 300g bulgur wheat
- 2 green bell peppers, chopped
- 1 scotch bonnet pepper, chopped
- 2 tablespoons coconut oil
- 1 can coconut milk
- 2 spring onions, chopped
- 1 garlic cloves, minced
- 1 seasoning cube
- 1 tablespoon curry
- 250g green beans
- 2 cups stock
- Salt to taste

Method

- Blend all the peppers, garlic, onion, and boil for 20 minutes in a saucepan, add coconut oil and fry up the chicken then add salt. Cook for 10 minutes or till chicken is cooked. Add blended pepper, coconut milk, then season with curry and seasoning cube.
- Add the green beans and cook for about 5 minutes or till beans is cooked. Remove beans and chicken from the curry sauce and set aside. Add stock and a cup of water to the curry sauce, bring to boil and add rinsed bulgur wheat. Cook for 25 minutes or till bulgur wheat is cooked. Garnish with sliced tomatoes and serve with green beans and chicken.

6. Sweet Potato Mash and Pan-fried Salmon

Serves 5 to 6

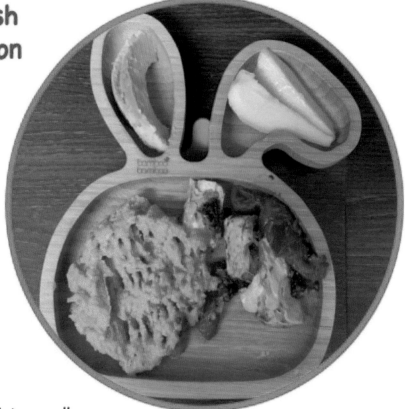

Ingredients

- 500g sweet potatoes
- 5 salmon fillets
- 1 teaspoon black pepper
- 1 teaspoon thyme
- 1 clove garlic, crushed
- 1 teaspoon ground ginger
- 1 teaspoon black pepper
- 1 tablespoon olive oil
- 3 whole tomatoes, halved
- Salt

Method

- Peel sweet potatoes and cut into smaller bits. Rinse well. In a pot, add sweet potatoes, water, and salt. Allow to cook for 20 to 25 minutes or till very soft. Mash sweet potatoes and set aside.
- While cooking the sweet potatoes, heat up olive oil in a pan. In a bowl, combine all spices and spread over salmon. Pan-fry salmon with skin side down for 13 to 15 minutes. Once salmon is cooked, add tomato to the pan and fry for 3 to 5 minutes. Serve salmon with tomatoes and mash.

7. Quinoa Bake with Yoghurt and Berries

Serves 6

Ingredients
- 1 cup quinoa
- 1 can black beans
- ½ cups oats flour or breadcrumbs
- 2 tablespoons tomato paste
- 1 teaspoon garlic powder
- 1 teaspoon hot sauce (optional)
- 1 teaspoon Smoked paprika
- Salt
- Pepper
- Strawberries, to serve
- Yoghurt, to serve

Method
- Add quinoa and 2 cups of water to pot and cook for 15 minutes. Drain excess water and set aside to cool. Add black beans to a bowl and mash with a fork or potato masher.
- Add quinoa, breadcrumbs or oats flour, hot sauce, tomato puree, garlic powder, paprika, salt and pepper. Mould into small balls, spray baking tray or line with baking sheet and bake for 25 mins at 180 degrees.
- Serve with strawberries and yoghurt.

8. Fried Rice Served with Egg and Cucumber (V)

Serves 5 to 6

Ingredients
- 300g rice
- 1 tablespoon curry powder
- 1 teaspoon thyme
- 1 onion, chopped
- 2 cups mixed veggies
- 3 tablespoons cooking oil
- 1 teaspoon white pepper
- 1 teaspoon black pepper
- 2 cups stock
- 1 seasoning cube
- 3 boiled eggs, to serve
- Cucumber, to serve

Method
- Cook rice in stock and one cup of water for 20 minutes, or till rice is cooked.
- Heat up oil in a pan, add chopped onion, thyme, white pepper and black pepper and fry for 3 to 5 minutes. Add mixed vegetables and seasoning cube. Fry for a few minutes.
- Add the cooked rice to the veggie stir-fry, mix till combined. Add splash of water, cover, and allow to simmer on low heat for 10 minutes. Serve with boiled eggs and cucumber.

9. Avocado and Egg Salad

Serves 2

Ingredients

- 1 medium avocado, diced
- 1 boiled egg, diced
- 2 medium tomatoes, diced
- 1 small cucumber, diced
- Salt
- Pinch of black pepper
- 1 teaspoon lemon juice

Method
Combine all ingredients and mix. Serve.

10. Amala, Ewedu and Fish

Serves 2

Ingredients

- 1 cup yam flour
- 1 cup jute leaves (ewedu), chopped
- ¼ cup ground crayfish
- Salt

Method
- Boil a cup of water in a saucepan, add jute leaves and allow to cook till soft for 10 minutes. Take off heat and blend till almost smooth. Return

back to heat; add salt and ground crayfish, mix properly. Add salt and cook for 5 minutes.

- Meanwhile, bring 2 cups of water to boil, add the yam flour and turn using a turner or wooden turning spoon. Keep turning till the flour has absorbed the water and without lump. If too thick, add water and allow to cook for 5 minutes, continue turning for another 5 to 7 minutes or till completely cooked. Serve with ewedu.

11. Penne and Spinach Sauce Served with Pears

Serves 6

Ingredients

- 300g penne, cooked and set aside
- Spinach 600g
- 3 red bell peppers
- 3 scotch bonnets
- 1 onion
- 1/3 cup olive oil
- ¼ cup ground crayfish
- 350g smoked mackerel
- 1 seasoning cube

Method

- Roughly chop bell pepper, scotch bonnet and onion in a blender or food processor.
- Heat up oil and add pepper mix. Cook for 5 to 10 minutes or till cooked; add crayfish, smoked mackerel, seasoning cube and salt. Mix all together and cook for another 5 minutes. Add in spinach and allow to simmer for a few minutes before serving with penne.

12. Shepherd Pie Served with Orange and Yoghurt

Serves 7

Ingredients

- 700g mashed potatoes
- 500g lamb minced
- 1 medium onion, chopped
- 200g tomatoes, chopped
- 3 carrots, thinly grated
- 200g frozen peas
- 2 tablespoons coconut oil
- 300ml beef stock or any stock available
- 1/4 cup all-purpose flour
- 1 teaspoon Thyme

Method

- Preheat oven 200'C/fan
- Add the onions, carrots, and thyme together. Cook and stir occasionally until vegetables are tender, or for about 10 minutes.
- Add flour and tomato into the vegetable mixture; cook and keep stirring for another 1 minute. Add lamb mince while cooking and keep stirring occasionally for 6 to 8 minutes until it's no longer pink. Finally, add the stock, let it boil and simmer for about a minute.
- Set beef filling aside.

For the mash:

- Add potatoes in a large pot and cover by 1 inch with salted water. Cook for about 20minutes or until potatoes are done. Drain water and mash the potatoes with 85g butter and 3 tablespoons of milk.

- Place the mince in an oven-proof dish, top it with the mash and ruffle with a fork. Bake for 20 to 25 minutes until the top changes colour and the mince starts bubbling through the edges.
- You can also free the pie into sections and bake anytime you wish.

13. Okra soup

Serves 7

Ingredients
- 700g Okra, chopped
- 350g mackerel fish, or any fish of choice
- ¼ cup ground crayfish
- 1 tablespoon Locust beans (optional)
- ¼ cup palm oil
- 700g spinach
- 1 seasoning cube
- 1 scotch bonnets
- 1 onion
- Salt to taste

Method
- In a blender or food processor, roughly chop scotch bonnet and onion and set aside.
- Add fish to a pot and cover with water, add salt and seasoning cube, cover and allow to cook for 20 minutes or till fish is cooked. Add chopped pepper mix, crayfish, locust beans and palm oil. Allow to cook for 7 minutes. Add okra.
- Taste for salt, cook for 5 minutes and serve with Eba (garri cooked with hot water) or amala (see Lunch 10 for this).

14. Broccoli Pesto Pasta with Mackerel

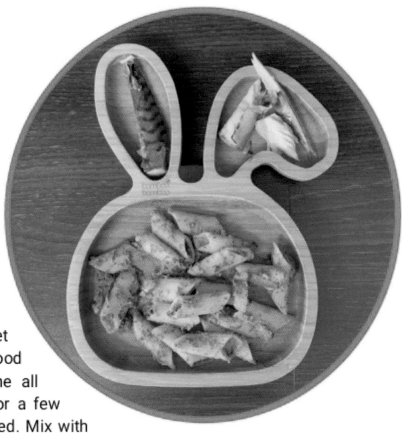

Serves 4

Ingredients

- 250g penne
- 1 cup broccoli, chopped
- 1 clove garlic
- 1/3 cup parmesan cheese
- 1/3 cup olive oil
- Pinch of salt
- 1 handful fresh basil
- 2 cups cooked mackerel fillet

Method

- Cook pasta according to packet instruction and set aside. In a food processor or blender, combine all other ingredients and pulse for a few seconds, add more oil if needed. Mix with pasta and serve with mackerel.

15. Prawns and Pea Rice Served with Grapes

Serves 6

Ingredients

- 2.5 cups rice
- 250g prawns
- 1 cup peas
- 1 teaspoon thyme
- 1 teaspoon curry powder
- 1 onion, chopped
- 1 cup stock (meat or vegetable)
- 2 tablespoons cooking oil
- 1 teaspoon black pepper
- Handful grapes

Method

- Add oil to a pot, add onion, thyme and curry powder. Fry for 3 minutes. Add stock, 2 cups of water, allow to boil and add rice. Cover pot and cook for 20 to 25 minutes.
- Add salt, peas and prawn and black pepper. Mix and allow to simmer for 10 minutes. Serve with grapes.

16. Lentil Curry and Potato (V)

Serves 6

Ingredients

- 250g split lentil
- 1 can coconut milk
- 1 teaspoon ginger paste
- ½ teaspoon ground turmeric
- 1 bell pepper, diced
- 1 onion, diced
- 1 medium potato, cubed
- 1 tablespoon curry powder
- 3 cups vegetable stock
- Salt
- Black pepper

Method

- Heat oil in a pot. Sauté onion for a few minutes, add pepper, ginger, turmeric potato, lentil, stock black pepper and salt. Cook for 25 minutes on medium heat. Stir in coconut milk and serve.

17. Chicken and Chips with Veggies and Yogurt Dip

Serves 5

Ingredients

- 4 medium potatoes
- Salt
- 2 tablespoons olive oil
- 1 teaspoon black pepper
- 200g broccoli and cauliflower floret
- 250g yogurt
- 10 grilled chicken wings

Method

- Peel potatoes and divide into wedges. In a bowl, combine potatoes, salt, olive oil and black pepper. Mix till well combined. Arrange wedges on a baking tray lined with baking sheet. Bake for 35 to 40 minutes, turning halfway through.
- Meanwhile steam broccoli and cauliflower floret and add a pinch of salt. Serve with potatoes, chicken wings and yoghurt.

18. Meatball and Avocado

Serve 6

Ingredient
- 500g minced meat/ ground meat
- 1 medium onion, minced
- 2 garlic cloves, minced
- 1 seasoning cube
- 1 tablespoon smoked paprika
- ¼ breadcrumbs (optional)
- 1 egg, whisked
- Salt

Method
- Preheat oven to 200 degrees. Combine all ingredients together, mix until just combined.
- Use an ice cream scoop—this will make the meat balls even—to scoop and mould into balls.
- Bake in the oven for 20 minutes or till no longer pink on the inside. Serve with avocado and toast or fries/chips.

19. Meatball Sauce and Spaghetti with Peas and Mango

Serves 6

Ingredients

- 18 meat balls (see recipe in Lunch 19)
- 4 cups blended pepper mix (tomatoes, bell pepper and scotch bonnet)
- 1 onion chopped
- 1 seasoning cube
- 1/3 cup cooking oil
- 1 teaspoon oregano
- 2 bay leaves

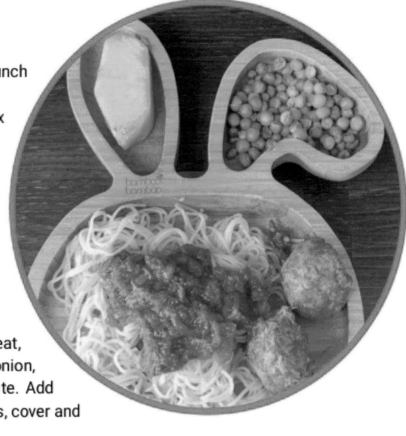

Method

- Heat a pan on medium heat, add oil. Once oil is hot, add onion, oregano and fry for one minute. Add blended pepper mix, bay leaves, cover and cook for 25 minutes.
- Add meat balls, salt, seasoning cube and allow to simmer on low heat for 15 minutes. Serve with pasta, rice or veggies.

20. Baked Potatoes, Cucumber, and Avocado Salad

Serves 2

Ingredients

- 1 medium cucumber, sliced
- ½ cup salad tomatoes, cut in halves
- 1 tin sweet corn
- 2 sausages
- 1 avocado, sliced
- 2 medium potatoes, cut into wedges
- 1 tablespoon mayonnaise
- 1 tablespoon lemon juice
- 1 tablespoon olive oil
- 1 teaspoon salt

Method

- Preheat oven at 200 degrees. In a bowl, combine oil, salt, and potato wedges. Arrange on a baking tray lined with baking sheet. Bake in the oven for 30 to 35 minutes turning halfway through. Halfway through, add in sausages.
- In a bowl, combine cucumber, tomatoes, sweet corn, mayonnaise, lemon juice and avocado. Toss together and serve with potato wedges and sausage.

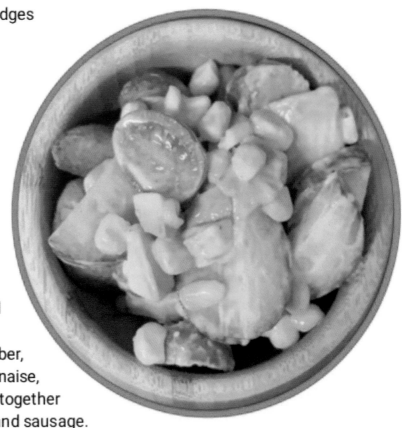

21. Creamy Salmon Pasta Bake

Serves 5 to 6

Ingredients

- 350g penne pasta
- 350g salmon fillet
- 3 spring onions, diced
- 2 cloves garlic, minced
- 2 tablespoon butter
- 2 tablespoons flour
- 2 cups milk
- Seasoning cube
- 1 teaspoon black pepper
- ½ cup grated parmesan (divide into 2)
- 3 tablespoons bread crumps

Method

- Cook pasta in salted water for 12 minutes or till al-dente. Drain and set aside. Meanwhile, reheat oven to 200 degrees. Heat a pan over medium heat. Add butter, spring onions, garlic, and cook for a few minutes. Add the salmon, salt and black pepper. Slowly add the flour to coat the fish, stir till well combined. Add milk and bring to a boil. Season with seasoning cube and cook till bubbly.
- Remove from heat and stir in half of the parmesan. Add in pasta and pour in a baking dish. Top with bread crumbs and remaining parmesan. Bake for 12 to 15 minutes or till the top is crispy.
- Tip: if the sauce is too thick after adding pasta, add some of the drained water from cooked pasta.

22. Cauliflower Mac n cheese

Ingredients

- 50g Macaroni
- 1 tablespoon plain flour
- 1 cup cauliflower, chopped
- 2 cup milk
- 3 tablespoon butter
- 1 cup Cheese – preferably cheddar
- 1 teaspoon black pepper
- Salt

Method

- Preheat oven. Cook pasta in salted water till al- dente. Remove from heat and drain. In a saucepan, melt butter, whisk flour into the butter, continue whisking till bubbly (about 1 minute). Gently add milk and continue whisking till bubbling. Add salt and pepper to taste.
- Add one cup of shredded cheese and whisk till smooth. Add pasta and cauliflower.
- Pour half the mac and cheese in a baking dish, top with half the remaining cheese, top with the remaining mac and cheese and finish off with the remaining cheese.
- Bake in the oven for 30 minutes or till crispy and bubbly, Serve.

23. Mango Rice Salad (V)

Serves 3

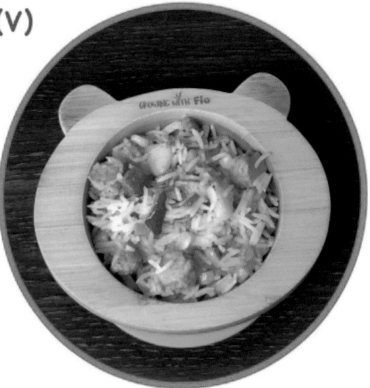

Ingredients
2 cups cooked rice
• ½ cup mango, diced
• 1 carrot, diced
• 1 bell pepper, diced
• 1 teaspoon freshly ground pepper
• 1 tablespoon lemon juice
• 3 tablespoons sweet corn
• 1 tablespoon cooking oil
• 2 grilled sausages, cut into bitable size
• 1 tablespoon cooking oil
• 1 small onion, diced
• Salt to taste

Method
- In a wok or pan, heat oil till hot. Add onion and pepper, stir fry for 5 minutes. Add ground pepper, salt and mix till well. Add carrot, rice, sweetcorn, and sausages mix till combined.
- Add the mango, lemon juice and serve.

24. Easy Tuna and Sweetcorn Wrap

Serves 2

Ingredients

- 1 small can sweet corn
- 1 can tuna
- 1 tablespoon mayonnaise
- Pinch of ground pepper
- 1 small cucumber, sliced
- 1 teaspoon lemon juice
- 2 tortilla wraps

Method

In a bowl, combine tuna, sweetcorn, black pepper, and lemon juice together. Spread over tortilla wrap. Fold wrap and cut into 2, serve with cucumbers.

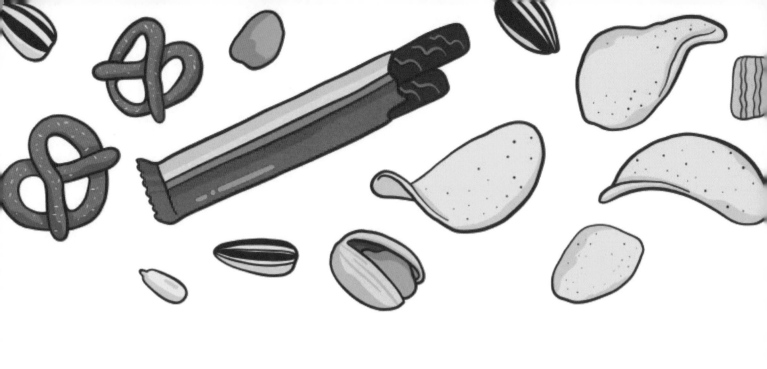

SNACK IDEAS

1. Fruit Kebab with Chocolate Dip

Ingredients
- 2 bananas
- 1 apple
- 2 clementines or tangerines
- Handful strawberries
- 2 kiwis
- Handful grapes
- Melted dark chocolate

Method
Cut all fruits into biteable sizes. Arrange on kebab sticks and drizzle with melted chocolate. Serve immediately or keep refrigerated.

2. **Fruit platter with any fruit of choice**
3. **Cheese board: cheese and crackers**
4. **Banana nice cream: a blend of frozen banana and yogurt with a dash of vanilla**
5. **Breadsticks and yoghurt dip**
6. **Corn on the cob**
7. **Cucumber and carrot stick with hummus dip**
8. **Fruit salad with colourful fruits of choice**
9. **Hard boiled eggs**

10. Rice cakes topped with mashed avocado
11. Banana slices topped with peanut butter
12. Pina colada popsicle: a blend of banana, pineapple and milk.
13. Peanut butter milkshake: a blend of milk, peanut butter, and banana
14. Strawberry and watermelon slush: a blend of watermelon, strawberries, and ice
15. Apple slices and peanut butter creamy dip: a mixture of peanut butter and and plain yoghurt
16. Yoghurt topped with strawberries
17. Plain crackers topped with cream cheese and jam
18. Fruit jelly, in any flavour of choice
19. Cucumber sandwich: sliced cucumber with a filling of chicken strips, and tomato slice.
20. Fruit and cracker pizza: crackers topped with cream cheese/ yoghurt and diced fruits.
21. Cheesy toast: toast with melted cheese.
22. Frozen yoghurt bite: yoghurt topped with fruits and frozen in cup cake tin
23. Apple pie
24. Strawberry tart

4-WEEK SAMPLE MEAL PLAN

WEEK 1

DAY	Breakfast	Lunch	Dinner	Snacks
Monday	English breakfast egg and beans	Grilled avo-tortilla wrap with cucumbers	Broccoli pesto pasta and mackerel	Apple and peanut butter dip
Tuesday	Berry milkshake	Broccoli and prawn rice	Lentil curry and potatoes	Pina colada popsicle
Wednesday	English breakfast egg and beans	Grilled avo-tortilla wrap with cucumbers	Broccoli pesto pasta and mackerel	Apple and peanut butter dip
Thursday	Breakfast muffin with fruits	Grilled chicken wings, plantain and grapes	Meatball sauce spaghetti and peas	Yoghurt topped with blueberries
Friday	Berry milkshake	Broccoli and prawn rice	Lentil curry and potatoes	Pina colada popsicle
Saturday	Banana pancakes, yoghurt and kiwi	Pepperoni pizza with veggies	Creamy salmon pasta bake	Cheese board
Sunday	Breakfast muffin with fruits	Grilled chicken wings, plantain and grapes	Meatball sauce spaghetti and peas	Yoghurt topped with blueberries

4-WEEK SAMPLE MEAL PLAN

WEEK 2

DAY	Breakfast	Lunch	Dinner	Snacks
Monday	Avocado toast with chicken and melon	Rice and beans with fish stew	Chicken, chips and veggies	Breadstick with yoghurt dip
Tuesday	Raspberry oats smoothie	Giant couscous and veggie medley	Shepherd pie	Strawberry and watermelon slush
Wednesday	Avocado toast with chicken and melon	Rice and beans with fish stew	Chicken, chips and veggies	Breadstick with yoghurt dip
Thursday	Raspberry oats smoothie	Giant couscous and veggie medley	Shepherd pie	Strawberry and watermelon slush
Friday	French toast and berries	Mexican pasta mix with fruits and egg	Avocado and egg salad	Banana nice cream
Saturday	Veggie fish cake	Jollof rice, chicken and avocado	Penne and spinach sauce	Fruit salad
Sunday	French toast and berries	Mexican pasta mix with fruits and egg	Avocado and egg salad	Banana nice cream

4-WEEK SAMPLE MEAL PLAN

WEEK 3

DAY	Breakfast	Lunch	Dinner	Snacks
Monday	Veggies egg frittata with bagel and tomatoes	Macaroni and chickpea casserole and steamed carrots	Amala and ewedu	Fruit jelly
Tuesday	Creamy banana oats and berries	Veggie coconut rice and eggs	Quinoa bake with yoghurt and berries	Cucumber and carrot with dip
Wednesday	Veggies egg frittata with bagel and tomatoes	Macaroni and chickpea casserole and steamed carrots	Amala and ewedu	Fruit jelly
Thursday	Creamy banana oats and berries	Veggie coconut rice and eggs	Quinoa bake with yoghurt and berries	Cucumber and carrot with dip
Friday	Egg and potato medley with strawberries	Seafood risotto with meat balls and fruits	Sweet potato mash and pan fried salmon	Any fruit of choice
Saturday	Oatmeal pancakes and yoghurt	Eba and egusi soup	Fried rice, eggs and cucumber	Any snack of choice
Sunday	Egg and potato medley with strawberries	Seafood risotto with meat balls and fruits	Sweet potato mash and pan-fried salmon	Any fruit of choice

4-WEEK SAMPLE MEAL PLAN

WEEK 4

DAY	Breakfast	Lunch	Dinner	Snacks
Monday	Grilled sandwich and fruits	Pasta in lentil sauce, mackerel and kiwi	Chilli con carne, mash and broccoli	Any snack of
Tuesday	Egg and avocado wrap	Beans and plantain	Curried bulgur wheat, chicken and green beans	Corn on the cob
Wednesday	Grilled sandwich and fruits	Pasta in lentil sauce, mackerel and kiwi	Chilli con carne, mash, and broccoli	Any snack of
Thursday	Egg and avocado wrap	Beans and plantain	Curried bulgur wheat, chicken and green beans	Corn on the cob
Friday	Mango lassi	Moi moi with steamed veggies	Grilled platter, sweet potato, mackerel and veggies	Rice cake topped with avocado
Saturday	Oatmeal pancake	Moi-moi with steamed veggies	Grilled platter, sweet potato, mackerel and veggies	Rice cake topped with avocado
Sunday	Mango lassi	Moi-moi with steamed veggies	Grilled platter, sweet potato, mackerel and veggies	Rice cake topped with avocado

ABOUT APRIL

As a weight-loss coach and food nutritionist, I am so particular about the food I eat. When I became a mother, food choices also became about my children. I was faced with the same questions that many mothers ask: how do I feed my baby with healthy meals when they are weaned? How do I ensure that my baby gets all the nutrients required for development through their food? By answering *this question*, I came across a wealth of resources. I experimented with different meals. Today, my children, Flo and Bryan, are better for it, eating healthy and growing stronger by the day.

While experimenting, I made a mess of food so that I can share this message of healthy cooking for babies with you. In this book, I share my years of experience planning and making healthy meals for my children. In my first book, *What Flo Eats*, I shared the kinds of foods to prepare your child for healthy cooking immediately when weaning. *What Flo Eats II*, takes off from where the first book stopped, providing more meals, even with vegetarian options. Though targeted at babies, many of these meals can be eaten by the entire family.

It is important to make sure that your growing children continue to get the right amount of nutrients they need to grow healthy. The best way to do this is to feed them balanced meals. Transform your child's menu from bland to wow, with a range of creative healthy food ideas that are sure to make your toddler eat every last bite. Just because it's healthy doesn't mean it can't be yummy! Flo and I are here to tell you that.

I'm also a baker, writer, traveller and music fan. Meanwhile, Flo, my healthy food-loving daughter made this book possible. ♥

My Favourite Weaning Products

Flo's Stay-Put Panda Bowl — *easy transition to adult plates*

Flo's Stay-Put Fish Plate — *easy transition to adult plates*

 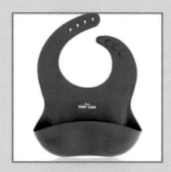  

www.growingwithflo.co.uk